Before using these books...

☞ A teacher/counselor manual is separately available for guiding students in the use of these workbooks.

✎ To prevent bleed-through, it is recommended that water-based, rather than spirit-based, markers or pens be used in this workbook.

Important

This book is not intended as a treatment tool or to be utilized for diagnostic or investigative purposes. It is not designed for and should not be recommended or suggested for use in any unsupervised, self-help or self-therapy setting, group or situation. Professionals who use this book are exercising their own professional judgement and take full responsibility for doing so.

The STARS LifeSkills Program

Teacher/Counselor Manual

Learning About Anger

Learning More About Anger

Knowing Yourself

Getting Along with Others

Respecting Others

How Drugs and Alcohol Affect Us

Knowing Yourself

Jan Stewart

Illustrated by Cecilia Bowman

ISBN 0-89793-311-7

© 2003 Jan Stewart and Hunter House

Design and layout Jinni Fontana © 2003 Hunter House

First U.S. edition published in 2003 by Hunter House.

For further information, contact Hunter House, Inc.

STARS: Steps to Achieving Real-life Skills

Knowing Yourself

Dear Student:

This workbook is part of a program to help you learn some real-life skills. You may already have some of these skills, and the information may just be a reminder or a review. If the information is new to you, then it is possible for you to learn skills and strategies that can help you for the rest of your life.

If you are unable to complete any section, leave it blank and come back to it later. If you are still unsure, ask your parent or guardian to assist you. If this is not possible, ask the person who gave you the workbook. On the next page is a glossary of words that are used in the workbook. Read this before you begin.

Please remember to have your parent or guardian fill out the last page.

Thank you for your cooperation.

Name of Student: _____

Adviser: _____

Assignment Date: _____

Completion Date: _____

Glossary

Aggressive—demanding rights without thinking about the rights of others

Confident—feeling sure of yourself

Dignity—a sense of worth, pride, or self-respect

Dilemma—a difficult problem to decide about

Free speech—the right to speak your mind or state your opinion in public

Goal—something you want to accomplish

Justice—fairness and true respect for all

Loyal—true or faithful

Monetary—relating to money

Symbol—something that represents another thing

Wealth—a lot of money or resources

Knowing Yourself

Values, Goals, Communication, and Expression

Knowing yourself requires that you take a close look at who you are and what you believe. It also means recognizing how you relate to other people. Communication skills are necessary if you want to satisfy your needs and wants. Understanding more about yourself will allow you to make decisions on what kind of person you want to be.

Values

Values are the standards or principles you live by, and they determine your goals.

Everything has some sort of value. Things might have a monetary value (for example, a pair of shoes may be worth $50). We also value things that are needed or are important to us like food, shelter, clothing, and safety. We value people we love. Some values, such as trust, are not visible or cannot be measured.

How do you get your values? Believe it or not, you have been forming your values since you were born. Our families have a major influence on our values. When your parents say, "Don't talk to strangers" or "Always tell the truth," they are sharing their values with you, so that you can develop your own values. You may also learn some values from school such as respecting others and the importance of working hard. Your values may change as you grow older and learn more about yourself.

If you were at a store and a friend asked you to steal something for him or her, your decision would likely be based on your values. If your parents tell you that stealing is wrong, and your friend is trying to encourage you to steal, you will have to decide what is more important. Should you do what you were taught or be loyal to your friend? Your decision will be based on your values.

Think of some of the values that are important to your family. How do family members demonstrate this value? **Write three values on the lines below and indicate how the value is shown.**

Family values	How the value is shown
e.g., honesty	Parents tell the truth and expect kids to as well
_____	_____
_____	_____
_____	_____
_____	_____

What Is Valuable to You?

Knowing about your values will help you get to know yourself better. **Put a check mark beside the ten values that seem most important to you.** Then pick the top five and number them with (1) being the most valuable and (5) being the least valuable. **Remember to pick your ten most important values first.**

_____ religion

_____ love

_____ free speech

_____ money

_____ education

_____ health

_____ creativity

_____ honesty

_____ good grades

_____ physical appearance

_____ a safe environment

_____ good friends

_____ change

_____ freedom

_____ financial success

_____ family members

_____ fame

_____ helping others

_____ equality

_____ shelter

_____ maturity

_____ dignity

_____ children

_____ career

_____ social life

_____ skill

_____ power

_____ wealth

_____ justice

_____ respect

_____ wisdom

_____ achievement

Now give the list on the following page to one more person, who may remain anonymous, and have him or her complete the exercise as well.

Sharing What Is Valuable

Note: You have been given this worksheet by someone who is learning about what values are. You can help this person by using this worksheet to tell the person what you value. **Put a check mark beside the ten values that seem most important to you.** Then pick the top five and number them with (1) being the most valuable and (5) being the least valuable. **Remember to pick your ten most important values first.**

_____ religion

_____ love

_____ free speech

_____ money

_____ education

_____ health

_____ creativity

_____ honesty

_____ good grades

_____ physical appearance

_____ a safe environment

_____ good friends

_____ change

_____ freedom

_____ financial success

_____ family members

_____ fame

_____ helping others

_____ equality

_____ shelter

_____ maturity

_____ dignity

_____ children

_____ career

_____ social life

_____ skill

_____ power

_____ wealth

_____ justice

_____ respect

_____ wisdom

_____ achievement

How are your lists similar? How are they different? What are some reasons for the differences?

_____

_____

The Fire

Imagine that you and your family are ordered to evacuate your home because an out-of-control fire is raging in your neighborhood. You and your family must move to safer ground and there is no guarantee that you will be able to return again. You have enough time to grab ten items that are important to you.

If you were put into this situation, what items would you take?

1. _____

2. _____

3. _____

4. _____

5. _____

6. _____

7. _____

8. _____

9. _____

10. _____

You are told that space is limited on the evacuation bus so you must take only five of your choices. What will they be?

1. _____

2. _____

3. _____

4. _____

5. _____

Discuss why you chose the items you did.

_____

_____

_____

_____

_____

_____

_____

_____

Explain the fire situation to someone else. What would that person take?

1. _____
2. _____
3. _____
4. _____
5. _____
6. _____
7. _____
8. _____
9. _____
10. _____

Why did he or she choose the items to take away before the fire?

_____

_____

_____

_____

_____

_____

_____

_____

_____

What were his or her choices on the second list?

1. _____
2. _____
3. _____
4. _____
5. _____

How did this activity help you to discover your values? Why would different people choose different items?

_____

_____

_____

_____

_____

_____

_____

Your Personal Flag

Design a flag to represent yourself.

1. In the top right box, draw something that you are good at.

2. In the top left box, draw the values that you would never change or give up.

3. In the bottom right box, draw something that you would like to achieve for yourself.

4. In the bottom left box, draw a picture that represents one value your whole family would believe in.

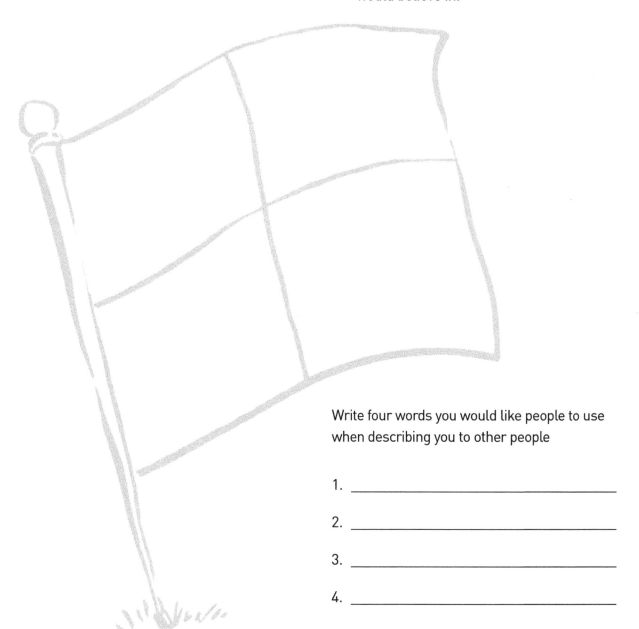

Write four words you would like people to use when describing you to other people

1. _____

2. _____

3. _____

4. _____

What Do You Value in a Friend?

Imagine that you and your family have just recently moved to a new city. You arrive at school and meet ten new people. Who would you like to be friends with? **Read each of the descriptions below and order them from 1–10 (1 = the person you would most like to have as a friend, 10 = the person you would least like to have as a friend).**

_____ **Brilliant Bobbi:** Bobbi does extremely well in school and is very interesting. Bobbi reads a lot and has a lot of knowledge on many subjects.

_____ **Attractive Ali:** Ali always dresses well and wears the trendiest clothes. Ali looks like a model, and other people always talk about Ali's good looks.

_____ **Trusting Terry:** Terry is honest, considerate, and always tells the truth. Terry never talks behind other people's backs and is very respectful.

_____ **Joking Jamie:** Jamie is the class clown and always seems to get everyone going. Jamie can always get a laugh out of people even when they are feeling down.

_____ **Risk-taking Rey:** Rey is adventurous, outgoing, and loves a challenge. Rey is willing to try all sorts of different things.

_____ **Quiet Qiao:** Qiao does a lot of thinking and keeps many opinions inside. Qiao is easygoing, considerate and doesn't like a lot of attention.

_____ **Artistic Andi:** Andi is good at designing, drawing, painting, and creating new things. Andi has a lot of innovative ideas and fun projects to work on.

_____ **Sporty Sam:** Sam is on just about every school team there is. If there is a sport or game to play, Sam does it.

_____ **Popular Pat:** Pat is a member of the "in" crowd. Pat has a lot of friends and is always asked to go out with others. Pat is very friendly and likes to do a variety of things.

_____ **Rich Ricky:** Ricky has just about every CD, computer game, video game, and sports equipment you could imagine. Ricky lives in a huge house with a swimming pool, pool table, sauna, and hot tub. Ricky loves to have friends come over.

Responses

Make a list of who you would most like to be friends with (#1) to the person you would least like to be friends with (#10).

1. _____

2. _____

3. _____

4. _____

5. _____

6. _____

7. _____

8. _____

9. _____

10. _____

What did this exercise teach you about your values? What do you value in a friend?

_____

_____

_____

_____

_____

If you had to come up with one word to describe yourself as a friend, what would it be?

_____

How would you describe yourself?

_____

_____

_____

_____

_____

Your Self-Talk

Sometimes the words you say inside your head can really help you out. Athletes use self-talk to help them win events. Self-talk is just a positive way to encourage yourself and give yourself confidence.

Say things like:

- I can do it.

- I can be strong.

- I can make a good choice.

- I know what I am doing.

- I am good at lots of things.

Everyone needs some confidence. Being able to compliment yourself is a good skill to have.

Practice saying **"I CAN."**

People can have many different skills that they can be proud of. It might be taking care of a pet, playing an instrument, telling a story, writing a poem, drawing a picture, playing a sport, or fixing a machine.

What can you do? List some things that you can do.

1. _____

2. _____

3. _____

4. _____

5. _____

6. _____

7. _____

8. _____

9. _____

10. _____

Not everyone can do what you can do!

Write Some Positive Self-Talk

Fill in the bubbles with positive self-talk that you could use to help yourself in the following situations:

1. You're about to take a final exam.

2. You're playing in a tournament final, and your team is losing.

3. Your friend was in an accident and has been taken to the hospital.

4. You failed a test in your worst subject.

5. You have just started working on a project for school worth 50 percent of your grade, and the due date is in two days.

6. You need to fix your bike in an hour, or you can't go out with your friends.

Bag It

If you were to put three objects into a bag that would show who you are, what would they be? The items should reveal what you enjoy, what you do best, or what you believe. They might be things you have at home. **Write the three things in the bag below.**

1.

2.

3.

Why did you pick each one?

_____

_____

_____

_____

_____

_____

What do the items say about you?

_____

_____

_____

_____

_____

_____

Advertise Yourself

You have probably seen lots of ads in your life. Some have caught your eye and some you probably can't even remember. Now think about yourself. What are some of your personal qualities that stick out? **Design an ad to advertise yourself.** If you have a magazine nearby, flip through it and notice what is eye-catching in an ad. You can use this ad and modify it, or you can design one without any help. Remember, keep it positive and make it eye-catching. We want to notice you.

Write your ad in the box below. It should fill the whole box.

How I See Myself

Evaluate yourself by putting a check in the appropriate box: never, sometimes, often, or always. It's difficult to evaluate yourself, but try to be honest and accurate.

I am...	Never	Sometimes	Often	Always
confident	☐	☐	☐	☐
friendly	☐	☐	☐	☐
happy	☐	☐	☐	☐
athletic	☐	☐	☐	☐
angry	☐	☐	☐	☐
thoughtful	☐	☐	☐	☐
trusting	☐	☐	☐	☐
responsible	☐	☐	☐	☐
lonely	☐	☐	☐	☐
popular	☐	☐	☐	☐
healthy	☐	☐	☐	☐
jealous	☐	☐	☐	☐
sad	☐	☐	☐	☐
aggressive	☐	☐	☐	☐
brave	☐	☐	☐	☐
cooperative	☐	☐	☐	☐
likable	☐	☐	☐	☐
competitive	☐	☐	☐	☐
clumsy	☐	☐	☐	☐
shy	☐	☐	☐	☐
worried	☐	☐	☐	☐
helpful	☐	☐	☐	☐
intelligent	☐	☐	☐	☐
artistic	☐	☐	☐	☐
bored	☐	☐	☐	☐

Draw Your Personal Constellation

A constellation is a group of stars in the sky that forms a shape. One way to think about people who are important to you is to imagine if each one were a star. What kind of constellation would they make?

List the people who mean something to you and write what you value most about them.

Example:

PERSON	WHAT YOU VALUE MOST
Mom	sense of humor
Sister	someone to shop with

Add as many people as you would like to your own list.

PERSON	WHAT YOU VALUE MOST
_____	_____
_____	_____
_____	_____
_____	_____
_____	_____
_____	_____
_____	_____
_____	_____

The following is an example of one person's constellation.

Now make your own constellation, including the people you just listed. Your constellation can make any shape you want and the stars can be any size or shape you want.

What picture or shape do all of your stars make together? Why did you choose this shape?

_____

_____

_____

_____

_____

Meet a Star

If you could meet a famous person either from the past or the present, who would it be? It can be any person you are familiar with from TV, movies, books, sports, music, or somewhere else.

Who would you like to meet? _____

What quality do you like most about her or him? _____

_____

If you met this star, what would be one question you would like to ask? _____

_____

If you could have one quality that this star has, what would it be? _____

_____

Is there one quality this star has that you would not want? _____

_____

Draw a picture of what your meeting with this star would look like in the space below.

The Way It Used to Be

1. What was his or her family like?

_____

2. What did he or she do for fun?

_____

3. What was school like?

_____

4. What chores/work did he or she have to do at home?

_____

5. What work did he or she do outside of home?

_____

6. What is one thing that you have that he or she didn't have as a teen?

_____

7. What is one thing he or she had as a teen that you don't have?

_____

8. What does he or she believe is the biggest difference between teens today compared to teens thirty years ago?

_____

Name of person you interviewed:

_____

Goal Setting

Setting a goal for yourself can help you think about what you would like to accomplish. Working towards that goal can give you confidence. Sometimes the goal may take a long time to accomplish and sometimes just a short time. Goals can be related to school, careers, sports, home projects, hobbies, or even physical appearance. Knowing what you want in life helps to provide you with direction and purpose.

What do you plan to do in the present? (These are your short-term goals.)

1. _____

2. _____

3. _____

What do you plan to do in the future? (These are your long-term goals.)

1. _____

2. _____

3. _____

In some cases, goals can be broken down into smaller goals. If your goal was to finish the 100-meter sprint in less than 20 seconds and it now takes you 35 seconds, you could break this goal into even smaller parts. For example, in the first week, your goal might be to get under 30 seconds three tries out of five. The next week you could work at getting under 28 seconds three times out of four. You could continue to break this into smaller parts so that you can celebrate some success along the way. Giving yourself a reward for success is also a great idea.

If your goal was to hand in a ten-page essay in a month, what could your smaller goals be?

1. _____

2. _____

3. _____

4. _____

Drawing Your Goals

Start with a picture of your final goal.

Now draw snapshots of your steps leading up to your final goal.

Step 1   Step 2

Step 3   Step 4

Rewards

Some people say that if they achieve their goals then they will go out to a movie or buy themselves a CD. People have their own ways to reward themselves. Sometimes, just taking a break is a reward. What would be some reasonable rewards you could give yourself when you accomplish a goal?

In the space below, draw your rewards.

Decision Making

Learning how to work through a problem and making informed decisions will help you gain a better understanding of who you are and how you think. By thinking about your past decisions and using all of the information available to you, you will find it easier to work through difficult situations.

To help guide you through the process, remember the word **SOLVE.** This is what it stands for:

S   **State** the problem

O   **Outline** your options

L   **List** the good and bad points of the options you like

V   **Visualize** the outcome

E   **Execute** your plan and **evaluate** your results

State the problem. When you have a decision to make, state what the problem is and try to be as specific as possible. For example, suppose you were accused of stealing something in a store. You didn't steal anything, and you need to respond to the clerk without the situation getting out of control.

Outline your options. Decide what you can do about the situation. Brainstorm all the ideas you can think of. For example, in private you could approach the person accusing you and explain the situation; or you could call your par-

ents to explain things to them. Think of all the ideas you can, and, if it's possible, write them down.

List the good and bad points of the options you like. Pick the options that you think are the best. Maybe some of your options could be changed or joined together into an even better idea. At this time you do not have to be worried about details.

Visualize the outcome. Go over some of your responses to the problem situation. Think to yourself: "What will happen if I...?" Think ahead and try to picture what the result will be if you choose a particular option. "How will it affect what I feel, need, and want? How will it affect others? How will it relate to what I and my family believe?" Once you have thought about the outcome of using your options, pick the best one and decide what you will do.

Execute your plan and evaluate your results. The final steps are to act out your plan and then see if you made a decision that helped you or not. Ask yourself, "Did things turn out the way I thought? Is the solution better than if I hadn't done anything? What are the consequences of this solution?" Remember, just like athletes need to practice their sport over and over again, you may need some practice to find the best solution to solve the problem. However, with a lot of practice, you can be a good decision maker!

Try using the SOLVE method to solve any of the following problems. **Choose one of the following problem situations and circle the number beside it.**

1. A friend you know is trying to hurt herself and has told you to keep it a secret.

2. A friend just invited you to go out, but you already said you would work.

3. A friend of yours wants you to lie to the teacher so that he doesn't have to stay for detention.

4. For the big science project the teacher is making you work with a girl who always pushes you around.

5. Your brother or sister is stealing money from your parents to buy cigarettes and your parents suspect you.

After you have chosen one situation, follow the SOLVE steps to work through the problem. You may need to use your imagination to decide on the entire situation.

S (STATE the dilemma) _____

_____

O (OUTLINE your options) _____

_____

L (LIST the good and bad points of the options you like)_____

_____

V (VISUALIZE the outcome)_____

_____

E (EXECUTE your plan and EVALUATE the results) _____

Which part was the most difficult to do?_____

Explain why it was difficult. _____

_____

Expressing Yourself

Everyone expresses themselves in different ways. Words, speech, drama, art, music, dance, and other creative activities can help you communicate a message to others. What would you like people to know about you? Think about what you believe in and what you enjoy. What symbols or illustrations could show the kind of person you are? **Express your ideas and thoughts using a variety of forms.**

Graffiti

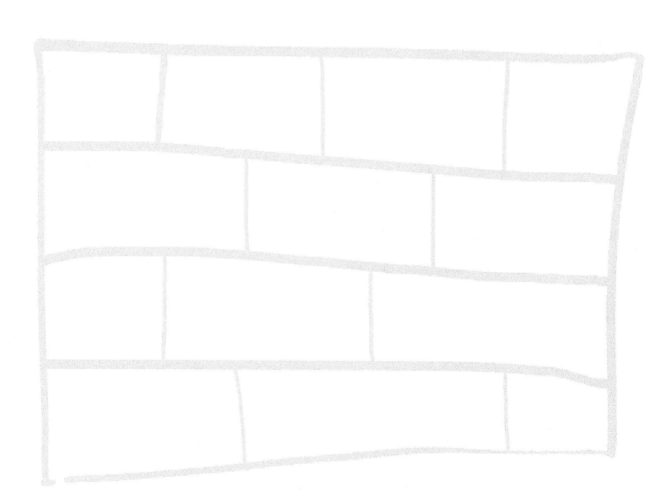

On a T-Shirt

FRONT

BACK

In a Poem

_____

_____

_____

_____

_____

_____

_____

In a Letter

Dear _____,

_____

_____

_____

_____

_____

_____

Your Friend _____

On a Sign or Billboard

As a Painting

As a Tattoo

Others recognize and often admire people who are able to express themselves using a positive or productive approach. **List some other ways you might try expressing yourself.**

_____

_____

_____

_____

Journal Writing—Reflecting

Take a moment to think about the work you have done in this workbook. **Jot down some words about how you felt working on this workbook.** From there, use a sentence starter to write about what you have accomplished. Pick the sentence starter that you like and write a paragraph about anything you want. This is a chance for you to be creative and to write something for yourself. Use the space below and a separate sheet if necessary.

If you are better with pictures, feel free to draw a picture.

Sentence Starters

In my life, I can…

I have the power to change…

In the future, I would like…

This year, I would like…

_____

_____

_____

_____

_____

_____

_____

Knowing Yourself

Parents/Guardians

It would be helpful if you could review and comment on the work that your child has done in this workbook. We encourage students to work with their parents on certain sections and we thank you for your cooperation. We hope that your child has had a chance to examine their behavior and to plan positively for the future. This unit has exposed students to a lot of information which we hope could be reviewed at home. We greatly appreciate your partnership in this project.

Comments: _____

_____

_____

_____

_____

_____

_____

Please feel free to contact the student's advisor or the person who assigned this workbook if you have any other questions or concerns.

Students

Now that you have completed the workbook, we urge you to provide some comments. Please comment on anything positive, e.g. "What did you like about it?" Also comment on what you did not like. If you have any suggestions, we would also like to hear them. **Congratulations for all your hard work!**

Comments: _____

_____

_____

_____

_____

_____

Printed in the USA
CPSIA information can be obtained
at www.ICGtesting.com
JSHW060049150824
68134JS00031B/2696